AMERICAN HEROES

CESAR
CHAVEZ

By
Abigail Fitzwild

HOUGHTON MIFFLIN   BOSTON

Cover Background Image: United Farm Workers march during the grape boycott, 1976

Printed in Hong Kong

ISBN-13: 978-0-618-67741-2
ISBN-10: 0-618-67741-0

4 5 6 7 8 9 10 - RRD - 12 11 10 09 08 07

Contents

CHAPTER 1

Early Years

Cesar Chavez knew how hard life was for farm workers. When he was a boy, his family moved from farm to farm to find work. Cesar went to a different school each time they moved. At times, he did not go to school so he could earn money.

Cesar never forgot these hardships. He spent his life fighting for better pay and working conditions for farm workers.

Chavez led farm workers in demanding better living and working conditions. Many joined in his fight.

▼

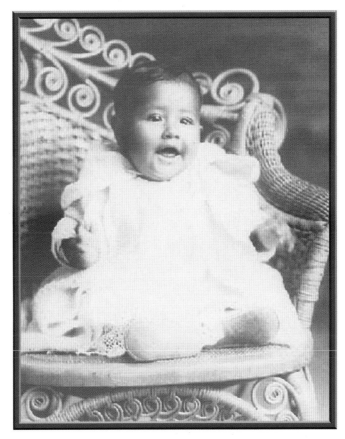

▲ This picture shows Cesar when he was a baby.

Cesar was born near Yuma, Arizona, in 1927. His parents had a strong influence on him. Each of them had come to the United States from Mexico as a child. Cesar's father was a farmer. He also ran a small grocery store and garage.

Cesar's father taught him the importance of hard work and **diligence.** His mother taught him to think about others. She also showed Cesar that talking, not fighting, was the way to solve problems.

◄ Young migrant children worked hard and for as many hours as adults.

In the 1930s, hard times hit the United States. Millions of people lost their jobs. Banks and businesses closed. The Chavez family lost their farm and grocery store in Arizona.

In 1937, when Cesar was ten, the family moved to the Imperial Valley in southern California. The Imperial Valley is an important farming region. In California, the Chavez family became **migrant workers.**

Migrant workers move from farm to farm to find work. They harvest, or pick, crops such as fruits and vegetables. When workers finish harvesting one type of crop, they move to another farm for more work.

Workers spent long hours in the hot sun. Pay was low. Sometimes farm owners did not pay their workers at all.

Cesar (bottom row, far right) and his brothers and sisters traveled with their parents to farms in California.

▼

Like most migrant farm workers, the Chavez family usually lived in camps provided by farm owners. Living conditions were bad. There might be no running water or electricity. Sometimes there were not even any houses. Workers had to live in tents.

When Cesar's father saw how badly migrant workers were treated, he became very angry. He told his family to stop working. Cesar understood that it was important to stand up for workers' rights.

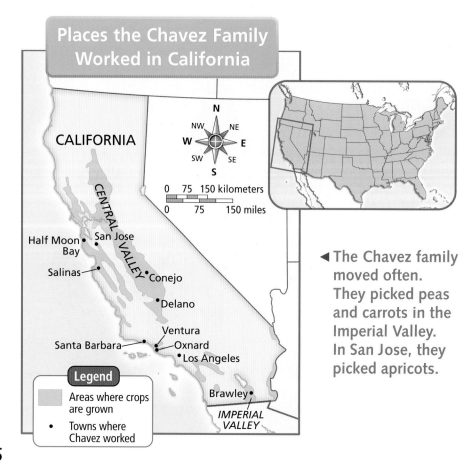

Places the Chavez Family Worked in California

CALIFORNIA

N
NW NE
W E
SW SE
S

0 75 150 kilometers
0 75 150 miles

CENTRAL VALLEY

Half Moon Bay
San Jose
Salinas
Conejo
Delano
Ventura
Santa Barbara
Oxnard
Los Angeles
Brawley
IMPERIAL VALLEY

Legend
Areas where crops are grown
Towns where Chavez worked

◄ The Chavez family moved often. They picked peas and carrots in the Imperial Valley. In San Jose, they picked apricots.

▲ Cesar graduated from eighth grade when he was 15 years old.

Because his family moved around so much, Cesar went to more than 30 different schools. There were times when he had to miss school to work. When Cesar and other migrant children did go to school, teachers and other students did not always treat them with respect. For example, Cesar's family spoke Spanish at home, but when Cesar spoke Spanish in class, he was punished.

Eighth grade was Cesar's last year in school. After that, he worked full-time to help earn money for his family. Cesar never stopped learning, however. He loved to read. He kept reading and learning for the rest of his life.

CHAPTER 2

Justice for All

Many people in California worked on farms. Mexican Americans, Asian Americans, African Americans, and many others worked hard under very difficult conditions.

Workers started early in the morning and worked all day. They might not be allowed to drink water before noon. There were no bathrooms. Workers who complained could lose their jobs.

This family picks grapes in California.
▼

There were no hot showers or soft beds, either. In some migrant camps, hundreds of people shared one water faucet for drinking, cooking, and washing.

Like his father, Chavez was unhappy about the unfair treatment he saw. He wanted all workers to be paid for their work. He believed that workers should be allowed to speak their own language. He also believed that all people should be treated equally.

When Chavez was 17, he joined the Navy. He wanted to get away from the unfair treatment of migrant farm workers. Chavez discovered, however, that Mexican Americans were often treated unfairly in the Navy, too.

▶ Chavez stayed in the Navy for two years.

▲ Many migrant workers lived in labor camps such as this one in Yuba City, California.

After Chavez left the Navy, he moved to San Jose, California. In 1948, he married Helen Fabela. He had known her since he was fifteen. Soon, Chavez went back to work on farms, picking crops, such as grapes and cotton. He and Helen lived in a cold, one-room shack. The shack was surrounded by mud, and had no running water or electricity.

In 1952, Chavez got a job with the Community Service Organization (CSO), a group that worked for **justice** for all people. Chavez wanted to help workers who were treated unfairly.

Part of Chavez's job was to speak to groups of people about working together to change things. Chavez was afraid he would not be a good speaker. He was wrong. People listened to him and agreed with what he said. Chavez learned he was a good leader and community **organizer.**

The CSO encouraged migrant workers to vote for laws that would improve working conditions.

▼

CHAPTER 3

Rights for Farm Workers

At the Community Service Organization, Chavez learned three things:

- There is power in knowledge.
- There is strength in numbers.
- Real change cannot be achieved through violence.

Chavez studied the work of Mohandas Gandhi in India and Dr. Martin Luther King, Jr. in the United States. Both had used nonviolent **protests** to bring important changes to their countries.

▲ Martin Luther King, Jr.

▲ Mohandas Gandhi

▲ Chavez spoke with many workers about standing up for their rights.

Chavez became the leader of the Community Service Organization in 1959. In that job, he helped thousands of people from Mexico become **citizens** of the United States. He helped more than ten thousand Mexican Americans sign up to vote. He also taught Mexican Americans about their rights in the United States and how to stand up for them.

Chavez continued to care about migrant workers' issues. He wanted to start a **labor union** to help farm workers win recognition of their rights.

13

▲ Dolores Huerta worked with Chavez to form the Farm Workers Association.

In 1962, Chavez left the CSO to form the Farm Workers Association. The FWA was a labor union. Acting as a group, workers have more power than they would alone. A union can make employers give workers better pay and working conditions.

Other people had tried to organize migrant farm workers into unions before, but getting people who moved a lot to join a group was hard. Farm owners had sometimes used violence to prevent workers from joining unions.

Chavez knew farm workers were not happy. They wanted better pay and living conditions. Workers also wanted to be treated with respect.

"Organizing is like picking grapes . . . one bunch at a time," Chavez once said. Traveling diligently from farm to farm, he asked workers to join his union. Little by little the union grew.

Chavez asked farm workers to join his union so that as a group they could fight for better working conditions.
▼

CHAPTER 4

Success!

Chavez was not the only one working to make things better in California. In 1965, a small union of grape pickers in Delano, California, went on **strike.** Workers strike, or refuse to work, to force business owners to make changes.

The Delano strikers asked Chavez's union for support. Chavez and his union agreed. In 1966, the two unions joined together to form the United Farm Workers (UFW).

Workers asked people from all over the United States to stop buying California grapes.
▼

▶ This poster says "Long Live the Strike" in Spanish.

The strike was hard for both the workers and the growers. Striking workers did not earn money. Grapes spoiled on the vines and growers could not sell them.

Growers tried to get the farm workers to end the strike. They sometimes used violence or had the strikers arrested.

Chavez, however, did not give up. He knew that going on strike was one way workers could use their **freedom of expression** to demand better treatment.

Chavez used nonviolent protests, such as strikes, to express workers' rights and win public support. Another important nonviolent action he used was a **boycott.** Chavez asked people all over the United States to refuse to buy grapes grown in California. He believed that if people knew how poorly the grape pickers were treated, they would want to help them.

Chavez was right, and the boycott was a success. Across the country, many people stopped buying California grapes to help the farm workers.

The California grape strike lasted for five years.
▼

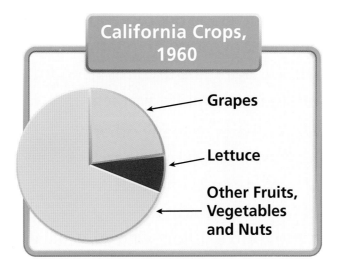

California Crops, 1960

Grapes

Lettuce

Other Fruits, Vegetables and Nuts

▲ By 1960, grapes were the largest fruit crop grown in California. A successful boycott of grapes would affect many farm owners.

Another form of nonviolent protest the UFW used was a **march.** Chavez and about 70 others walked from Delano to Sacramento, the California state capital. The 340-mile walk drew attention to the strike. Along the way, nearly 20,000 people joined the marchers.

After about five years, Chavez's diligence paid off. The grape growers signed an agreement with the United Farm Workers to give workers better pay and living conditions.

Soon after the grape boycott ended, Chavez began a lettuce boycott to help farm workers who picked lettuce. Again, he used his freedom of expression to speak out for workers' rights.

Chavez took part in many other protests. In 1975, he led a 1,000-mile march through California, from San Ysidro to Salinas. He wanted to tell farm workers about a new law that protected their right to form a union. Chavez walked every step of the 1,000 miles.

During a march, Chavez walked many miles each day. Each evening, he gave speeches.
▼

During the 1980s, Chavez learned about another problem that farm workers faced. Many farmers used pesticides to kill insects that damaged their crops. Pesticides also made workers sick. To draw attention to the danger of pesticides, Chavez went on a public **fast,** refusing to eat for 36 days.

Chavez worked hard to demand better conditions for migrant workers. He walked thousands of miles. He went on many fasts. He did not want to give up until he had succeeded.

This poster asks people to boycott lettuce and grapes grown in California.
▼

CHAPTER 5

We Remember Chavez

Cesar Chavez died in 1993. Throughout his life, Chavez worked to make things better for farm workers. He often said, *"Sí, se puede*—Yes, it can be done."

Today, farm workers earn more money and have better places to live. The United Farm Workers union that Chavez helped start still works to make life better for farm workers. Because of Chavez, people all over the United States know that farm workers need fair treatment.

▶ Cesar Chavez's grandson speaks at a celebration honoring his grandfather.

▲ Helen Chavez accepted the Presidential Medal of Freedom for her husband. The Medal is the highest honor a person in the United States can receive.

As a Mexican American leader, Chavez helped other Mexican Americans see that they had the same rights as all Americans. He believed that the United States should protect everyone's civil rights. Chavez showed people that they could work together for justice.

In 1994, President Bill Clinton awarded the Presidential Medal of Freedom to Cesar Chavez. Clinton said, "Cesar Chavez left our world better than he found it, and his **legacy** inspires us still."

The Cesar E. Chavez Foundation in La Paz, California, is an organization that continues Chavez's work. It trains people to become leaders. It also encourages people to be active citizens. Visitors to the foundation learn about the work of Chavez and the lives of farm workers.

Today, Chavez's birthday is a holiday in seven states. It is called the Cesar Chavez Day of Service and Learning. On this day, many people honor Chavez by taking part in community projects.

Chavez is honored with this statue in Cesar Chavez Plaza in Sacramento, California.
▼

▲ Chavez is remembered for saying
"*Sí, se puede* – Yes, it can be done."

Chavez's love for justice and belief in freedom of expression helped many people. He fought for the rights of the hardworking men and women who put food on our tables. He was never violent, even when violence was used against him. He never gave up.

Today, we remember Cesar Chavez as a hero who gave all he had to win recognition of workers' rights.

Cesar Chavez

Cesar Chavez brought change to farm workers all over the state and in other parts of the country. Use this map to find places that were important in Chavez's life.

Delano, 1966:
Chavez leads a march from Delano to Sacramento.

San Ysidro, 1975:
Chavez leads a 1,000-mile march through the Imperial and San Joaquin Valleys.

La Paz, 1988:
Chavez goes on a 36-day "Fast for Life" to protest pesticides.

Choose two locations on the map. How did the events there help Chavez succeed in helping farm workers?

▶ Chavez's fight for justice for migrant workers was honored with a postage stamp.

USA
37
CESAR E. CHAVEZ

OREGON

IDAHO

NEVADA

N
NW   NE
W ⬥ E
SW   SE
S

SACRAMENTO VALLEY

★ Sacramento

CALIFORNIA

SAN JOAQUIN VALLEY

1966 Chavez leads a march from Delano to Sacramento

Delano

• La Paz

1988 Chavez goes on a 36-day "Fast for Life" to protest pesticides

ARIZONA

1975 Chavez leads a 1,000-mile march through the Imperial and San Joaquin Valleys

PACIFIC OCEAN

0   75   150 kilometers
0   75   150 miles

San Ysidro   IMPERIAL VALLEY

27

MEXICO

Understanding Character Traits

People who work hard for a long time show **diligence**. Through his diligence, Cesar Chavez won recognition of migrant workers' rights.

To value **justice** means giving people the same treatment under the law. Cesar Chavez led farm workers in their fight for justice.

Having **freedom of expression** means being able to say and do what you believe is right. Cesar Chavez used his freedom of expression to speak out for workers' rights and to organize strikes and boycotts.

How do you use your freedom of expression?

▶ Chavez spoke at many meetings, marches, and protests throughout his life.

GLOSSARY

boycott refusing to buy something as a protest (p. 18)

citizen an official member of a country (p. 13)

diligence hard and long work (p. 3)

fast going without food to make a point (p. 21)

freedom of expression the freedom to say what you believe (p. 17)

justice equal treatment under the law (p. 11)

labor union an organization of workers who work together for better pay and conditions (p. 13)

legacy something passed down to younger people (p. 23)

march an organized walk taken by a group of people to make a point (p. 19)

migrant worker a person who goes from place to place in search of work (p. 4)

organizer someone who brings people together to accomplish a task or to meet a goal (p. 11)

protests action taken to show that people want change (p. 12)

strike refusal by workers to work to protest low pay, or poor working conditions (p. 16)

INDEX